IMPROVING
VOCABULARY

for ages 9-10

Andrew
Brodie

Introduction

All the activities in *Improving Vocabulary* are specifically designed to promote pupils' knowledge and use of an extensive range of words in their speaking and listening, reading and writing. This six book series provides a structured programme of activities, which will ultimately form invaluable practice for the English grammar, punctuation and spelling test at the end of Key Stage 2.

Research has shown that good use of vocabulary is vitally important for learning and that there is a clear link between a child's level of vocabulary at age five and his or her future success at sixteen or beyond. For good educational progress to be made, children need to experience high-quality language development activities.

Throughout the books, the vocabulary has been carefully selected for the designated age group and progression is also integral to the activities. The activity sheets are differentiated at three levels and are designed to be used by individuals or small groups working with an adult. **Teacher's notes** on each sheet provide guidance on how to get the most from the activity. In general, adults should encourage the children to respond to low-demand questions first before moving on to high-demand questions as they become more confident.

How to use the book and CD-ROM together

The revised National Curriculum Programme of Study for Years 5 and 6 indicates the importance of learning new vocabulary, particularly as part of the reading process. The Programme of Study states that 'teachers should continue to emphasise pupils' enjoyment and understanding of language, especially vocabulary, to support their reading and writing'. It also says 'there will continue to be a need for pupils to learn subject-specific vocabulary'. The Programme of Study for Writing states that pupils should be taught to draft and write by 'selecting appropriate grammar and vocabulary, understanding how such choices can change and enhance meaning'. The activities in this book provide opportunities for practising all of these aspects of the National Curriculum, as well as other important language development skills such as word categorisation.

The book has fifteen Key Activities, which can be projected on to a whiteboard for whole class use and photocopied/printed for display. Sharing the Key Activities either on screen or paper provides lots of opportunities for speaking and listening, for decoding words through a phonic approach, for reading and writing, and for satisfaction and enjoyment in shared success.

For each Key Activity there are three vocabulary sheets at different levels to enable you to differentiate across the ability range in your class. An animal picture at the top of the sheet indicates the level: the cat exercises are at the simplest level; the dog exercises are at the next level and the rabbit exercises are at the most advanced level. You may start off by giving some pupils the cat worksheet and then decide, on the basis of their success, to move them on to the dog worksheet. A similar approach could be taken with the dog and rabbit sheets.

The activity sheets are aimed at the following ability levels:
* Cat activity sheets are for pupils who may need **extra help**.
* Dog activity sheets are for pupils who are **progressing well**.
* Rabbit activity sheets are for **higher ability pupils**.

Andrew Brodie: Improving Vocabulary for ages 9-10 © Bloomsbury Publishing Plc 2012

Contents

Water

Water

Verbs

Nouns

Adjectives

Teacher's notes

Photocopy and cut out the Water heading and the category title cards to use in conjunction with the activities on the following three sheets. This activity provides lots of opportunities for speaking and listening and introduces important everyday vocabulary. The theme of Water is regularly visited during primary education: the emphasis in this Key Activity is on the creative use of words related to water rather than on the use of specialist scientific or geographical vocabulary.

Water

waterfall	torrent	flowing / surging	surfing
tumbling	gushing	clear	murky / stagnant
still	sparkling	powerful	cascade / cascading
fountain	bubbling	bubbly	waves / rolling
mighty	ocean	towering	fresh / white horses

Teacher's notes

Cut out the words and illustrations above and use them in conjunction with the category title cards from page 5. Use the cards created from this sheet as prompts for discussion to ensure that this is a speaking and listening activity as well as a reading activity. Encourage the children to talk about water using the vocabulary provided. Do they know what all the words mean? Are some of the words only applicable to the sea? Are some of the words only applicable to fresh water? Talk about the word 'gushing', pointing out that this can be used as a verb or as an adjective: The water was gushing over the edge of the cliff; the gushing water washed everything away. Can they find other words that can be used as either verbs or adjectives? Can they create oral sentences using some of the verbs, nouns and adjectives?

Andrew Brodie: Improving Vocabulary for ages 9-10 © Bloomsbury Publishing Plc 2012

Water

Word Bank

depth
meander   surging   rapids   clapping   meandering   shallow
deep   stagnant   flowing   ocean   slapping   white horses   still
surfing   crashing   waterfall   cascade   gushing   waves   clear
shallows   mighty   bubbly   sparkling   powerful
torrent   towering   tumbling
pounding   fountain   cascading   murky   fresh   bubbling   rolling

Write each of the words from the Word Bank in the correct section of the table.

Nouns	Adjectives	Verbs

Can you think of any extra words to write in the table?
Write two sentences. Use a verb, a noun and an adjective from the table in each one.

_____

_____

_____

_____

Teacher's notes

Discuss the words in the Word Bank in conjunction with the category title cards from page 5. Ensure that this is firstly a speaking and listening activity although it will provide practice in both reading and writing. Encourage the children to talk about water using the vocabulary provided. Do they know what all the words mean? Are some of the words only applicable to the sea? Are some of the words only applicable to fresh water? Talk about the word 'bubbling', pointing out that this can be used as a verb or as an adjective: The water was bubbling out of the ground; the bubbling water sparkled in the sunlight. Can they find other words that can be used as either verbs or adjectives? Can they create oral sentences using some of the verbs, nouns and adjectives? Once they are confident with the words ask them to write them in the correct section of the table. Finally, they can write two sentences each containing at least one of the verbs, one of the adjectives and one of the nouns.

Andrew Brodie: Improving Vocabulary for ages 9-10 © Bloomsbury Publishing Plc 2012

Name _____

Date _____

Water

depth surging rapids clapping meandering shallow
deep stagnant flowing ocean slapping white horses still
surfing crashing waterfall cascade waves clear
shallows mighty bubbly gushing sparkling powerful
pounding torrent towering tumbling
fountain cascading murky fresh bubbling rolling

Can you think of any extra words regarding water?
Write two nouns, two verbs and two adjectives.

_____

_____

_____

_____

_____

_____

Write three sentences describing a river.

_____

_____

_____

_____

_____

_____

_____

_____

_____

Teacher's notes

Discuss the words in the Word Bank in conjunction with the category title cards from page 5. Ensure that this is firstly a speaking and listening activity although it will provide practice in both reading and writing. Encourage the children to talk about water using the vocabulary provided. Do they know what all the words mean? Are some of the words only applicable to the sea? Are some of the words only applicable to fresh water? Talk about the word 'bubbling', pointing out that this can be used as a verb or as an adjective: The water was bubbling out of the ground; the bubbling water sparkled in the sunlight. Can they find other words that can be used as either verbs or adjectives? Can they create oral sentences using some of the verbs, nouns and adjectives? Once they are confident with the words ask them to write three well-structured sentences using nouns, verbs and, where appropriate, adjectives all related to the water in a river.

8

Andrew Brodie: Improving Vocabulary for ages 9-10 © Bloomsbury Publishing Plc 2012

Group words

Group words

Collective nouns

Teacher's notes

Photocopy and cut out these category title cards to use in conjunction with the activities on the following three sheets. Explain to the pupils that 'collective noun' is a term that is used instead of 'group word' - this is in itself a valuable example of specialist vocabulary.

Andrew Brodie: Improving Vocabulary for ages 9-10 © Bloomsbury Publishing Plc 2012

Group words

swarm	locusts	choir	singers	duo	trio
quartet	band	musicians	team	athletes	pod
dolphins	school	whales	company	actors	crew
sailors	crowd	people	host	angels	daffodils
regiment	soldiers	bouquet	bunch	flowers	keys
chest	drawers	row	houses		

Teacher's notes

Cut out the words and illustrations above and check that the children understand that the activity involves the use of group words and that these are also known as collective nouns. Try to ensure that this is a speaking and listening activity as well as a reading task. Encourage the children to think carefully about each of the items shown on the cards, helping them to match the plural items to the appropriate collective nouns. Note that some items could have several collective nouns associated with them: for example, the words duo, trio, quartet and band could all be used with 'musicians'. You may also wish to sort the vocabulary in other ways: for example into living and non-living things. Ask them to compose some oral sentences, which include a collective noun used appropriately. As an extension activity the pupils could write out a sentence, correctly composed and punctuated.

Andrew Brodie: Improving Vocabulary for ages 9-10 © Bloomsbury Publishing Plc 2012

Group words

Name _____

Date _____

Word Bank

range china   actors   fleet
         bundle   host   keys   daffodils   trio
mountains   athletes   choir
         ships   musicians   wad   angels
houses litter   people   team
         grass   sticks   set   clump
duo   singers   whales
money   wood   swarm   puppies
     pod   cubs   locusts
company   band   soldiers
      bunch   bouquet   sailors   quartet
school dolphins   crowd   drawers   regiment
                         row   chest   stack
crew   flowers

Insert an appropriate collective noun in each of the gaps below.

a _____ of puppies   a _____ of whales   a _____ of bees

a _____ of sailors   a _____ of flowers   a _____ of drawers

a _____ of ships   a _____ of mountains a _____ of houses

a _____ of soldiers   a _____ of people   a _____ of money

a _____ of singers   a _____ of musicians a _____ of athletes

Write two sentences, each of which contains a collective noun for a group.

_____

_____

Teacher's notes

Encourage the children to talk about the group words (collective nouns) listed in the Word Bank, creating oral sentences using these words appropriately with some of the animals, people or objects also listed. Note that some items could have several collective nouns associated with them: for example, the words duo, trio, quartet and band could all be used with 'musicians'. You may also wish to sort the vocabulary in other ways: for example into living and non-living things. When they are confident in using the words effectively, they can complete the other activities on the sheet.

Group words

Word Bank

range   china   actors   fleet

mountains   bundle   athletes   host   keys   daffodils   trio
                                                       choir

houses   litter   ships   people   musicians   wad   angels

grass   clump   team
duo   singers   sticks   set   whales

money   wood
      pod   cubs   train   swarm   locusts   puppies   troop

company   band   soldiers   quartet
      bunch   camels   bouquet   sailors

school   dolphins   crowd   drawers   regiment
                           row   chest   stack

crew   flowers   monkeys

Match all the collective nouns from the Word Bank with appropriate animals, people or objects. Can you think of other collective nouns?

_____   _____   _____

_____   _____   _____

_____   _____   _____

_____   _____   _____

_____   _____   _____

_____   _____   _____

_____   _____   _____

_____   _____   _____

_____   _____   _____

_____   _____   _____

_____   _____   _____

_____   _____   _____

_____   _____   _____

_____   _____   _____

Teacher's notes

Ask the children to talk about the group words (collective nouns) listed in the Word Bank, creating oral sentences using these words appropriately with some of the animals, people or objects also listed. Note that we are not seeking for children to know and remember all of the collective nouns. Instead, we are trying to encourage them to consider why certain vocabulary may have been chosen.

Word sorting: the heart, the solar system, sound

Non-fiction

Information

The heart

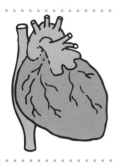

The solar system

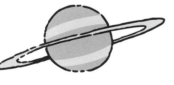

Sound

Teacher's notes

Photocopy and cut out the Non-fiction or Information headings and the category title cards to use in conjunction with the activities on sorting following three sheets. This type of categorisation activity can be very challenging for some children. All of the vocabulary listed will be of direct relevance to the pupils' work, now or in the future.

Word sorting: blood circulation, solar system, sound

space	travel	heart	lungs	oxygen	Saturn
Jupiter	orbit	Neptune	Venus	Mars	Uranus
satellite	sun	moon	Earth	Mercury	circulation
circulating	orbiting	carbon dioxide	blood	distance	hearing
sense	speed	vibration	volume	pitch	noise
muscles	planet	centre	source	light	healthy

Teacher's notes

Cut out the words and illustrations above and use them in conjunction with the category title cards from page 13. Ask the children to sort the words as though they appear in some non-fiction books: which words could be found in a book about blood circulation, which in a book about the solar system and which could be found in a book about sound? Could any of the words appear in more than one of the books? Could any of the words appear in all three books? As an extension activity, ask the children to compose orally two or three sentences that feature some of the words they have discussed. They could write out the best sentences.

Andrew Brodie: Improving Vocabulary for ages 9-10 © Bloomsbury Publishing Plc 2012

Word sorting: blood circulation, solar system, sound

Name _____

Date _____

Word Bank

accoustics galaxy space oxygen universe pump
Uranus vessels Saturn Mars
lungs circulation source Venus blood hearing travel
heart Neptune carbon dioxide satellite volume Mercury
noise orbit speed light Jupiter
orbiting pitch muscles moon sense circulating
vibration
sun distance planet centre healthy Earth

Look carefully at the words in the Word Bank. Which words could be found in a book about the heart, which in a book about the solar system and which could be found in a book about sound? Write the words in the correct places below. Some of the words could appear in more than one book.

The Heart	**The Solar System**	**SOUND**

On a separate piece of paper, write three sentences using some of the vocabulary relating to the heart, the solar system or sound.

Teacher's notes

Discuss the words above in relation to the category title cards from page 13. Do the children know what each word means? Can they think of any related words? For example, they could suggest the word 'vibrate' in relation to the word 'vibration'. Ask the children to sort the words as though they appear in some non-fiction books: Could any of the words appear in more than one of the books? Could any of the words appear in all three books?

Word sorting: blood circulation, solar system, sound

Name _____

Date _____

Word Bank

accoustics galaxy space oxygen universe Mars pump
Uranus vessels Saturn source Venus blood hearing travel
lungs circulation satellite volume Mercury
heart Neptune carbon dioxide light Jupiter
noise orbit speed muscles moon sense circulating
orbiting pitch vibration planet centre healthy arteries Earth
sun distance gravity asteroids
disease comets waste veins

Look carefully at the words in the Word Bank. Write the words in the correct book below. Some of the words could appear in more than one book.

The Heart

The Solar System

SOUND

Find some more vocabulary for each book.

Teacher's notes

Discuss the words above in relation to the category title cards from page 13. Do the children know what each word means? To find extra vocabulary for each list, the children could research in the school library or on the internet. They could also consider searching for words related to those on the list: for example, the word 'universal' is clearly related to the word 'universe'.

Andrew Brodie: Improving Vocabulary for ages 9-10 © Bloomsbury Publishing Plc 2012

Word sorting: machines, baking, flowers

Non-fiction

Information

Machines

Baking

Flowers

Teacher's notes

Photocopy and cut out the Non-fiction or Information headings and the category title cards to use in conjunction with the activities on the following three sheets. All of the vocabulary listed will be of great value to the pupils in their school work, now or in the future.

Word sorting: machines, baking, flowers

	mechanism	engine	powered	motor
cogs				
technology	computer	vehicle	dough	cooking
bakery	pastry	kneading	flour	flower
yeast	female	male	anther	filament
stamen	stigma	style	ovary	carpel

Teacher's notes

Cut out the words and illustrations above and use them in conjunction with the category title cards from page 17. Ask the children to sort the words as though they appear in some school books: which words could be found in a book about machines, which in a book about baking and which in a book about flowers? Some children will need a lot of help with the vocabulary related to flowers. Could any of the words appear in more than one of the books? Could any of the words appear in all three books? As an extension activity, ask the children to compose orally two or three sentences that feature some of the words they have discussed. They could write out the best sentences.

Andrew Brodie: Improving Vocabulary for ages 9-10 © Bloomsbury Publishing Plc 2012

Word sorting: machines, baking, flowers

Name _____

Date _____

Word Bank

computer
tool
cogs
engine
powered
loaf
motor
cakes
female
pastry
anther
yeast
mechanism
male
dough
filament
stamen
stigma
style
ovary
flower
carpel
degrees
printer
Celsius
biscuits
mechanical
bread
force
flour
rolling pin
technology
bakery
kneading
vehicle
cooking

Look carefully at the words in the Word Bank. Which words could be found in a book about machines, which in a book about baking and which could be found in a book about flowers? Write the words in the correct places below. Some of the words could appear in more than one book.

Machines
_____ _____
_____ _____
_____ _____
_____ _____
_____ _____
_____ _____
_____ _____

Baking
_____ _____
_____ _____
_____ _____
_____ _____
_____ _____
_____ _____
_____ _____

Flowers
_____ _____
_____ _____
_____ _____
_____ _____
_____ _____
_____ _____
_____ _____

On a separate piece of paper, write three sentences using some of the vocabulary relating to machines, baking and flowers.

Teacher's notes

Discuss the words above in relation to the category title cards from page 17. Do the children know what each word means? Some children will need help with the vocabulary related to flowers. Can they think of any related words? For example, they could suggest the word 'cookery' in relation to the word 'cooking'. Ask the children to sort the words as though they appear in some non-fiction books: Could any of the words appear in more than one of the books? Could any of the words appear in all three books?

Word sorting: machines, baking, flowers

Name _____

Date _____

wholemeal   computer   transmission   pollination
tool   loaf   cakes
cogs   engine   powered   motor
female   pollen
yeast   pastry   anther   filament
male   dough
mechanism
stamen   stigma   nutrients   style   ovary   flower   carpel
degrees   printer   Celsius   biscuits   mechanical   nutrition
force   gearing   bread   flour
technology   rolling pin
bakery   kneading   vehicle   cooking

Look carefully at the words in the Word Bank. Write the words in the correct book below. Some of the words could appear in more than one book.

Machines
_____ _____
_____ _____
_____ _____
_____ _____
_____ _____
_____ _____
_____ _____
_____ _____
_____ _____
_____ _____

Baking
_____ _____
_____ _____
_____ _____
_____ _____
_____ _____
_____ _____
_____ _____
_____ _____
_____ _____
_____ _____

Flowers
_____ _____
_____ _____
_____ _____
_____ _____
_____ _____
_____ _____
_____ _____
_____ _____
_____ _____
_____ _____

Find some more vocabulary for each book.

Teacher's notes

Discuss the words above in relation to the category title cards from page 17. Do the children know what each word means? To find extra vocabulary for each list, the children could research in the school library or on the internet. They could also consider searching for words related to those on the list: for example, the word 'mechanisation' is clearly related to the word 'mechanism'.

Andrew Brodie: Improving Vocabulary for ages 9-10 © Bloomsbury Publishing Plc 2012

Word sorting: music; gases, solids and liquids; Victorian Britain

Non-fiction

Information

Music

Gases, solids and liquids

Victorian Britain

Teacher's notes

Photocopy and cut out the Non-fiction or Information headings and the category title cards to use in conjunction with the activities on the following three sheets. Some of the vocabulary listed will be of great value in pupils' work on history or science, now or in the future.

Word sorting: music; gases, solids and liquids; Victorian Britain

guitar	performance	piano	orchestra
			violin
pitch	musician	opera	musical
			oxygen
water	ice	hydrogen	carbon dioxide
			boiling
freezing	melting	evaporating	condensing
			exhibition
discovery	invention	industrial	revolution
			empire
poverty	wealth	canals	strings
			percussion

Teacher's notes

Cut out the words and illustrations above and use them in conjunction with the category title cards from page 21. Ask the children to sort the words as though they appear in some school books: which words could be found in a book about music, which in a book about the gases, solids and liquids and which in a book about Victorian Britain? Could any of the words appear in more than one of the books? Could any of the words appear in all three books? As an extension activity, ask the children to compose orally two or three sentences that feature some of the words they have discussed. They could write out the best sentences.

Andrew Brodie: Improving Vocabulary for ages 9-10 © Bloomsbury Publishing Plc 2012

Word sorting: music; gases, solids and liquids; Victorian Britain

Word Bank

smog   railways   canals   melting   travel   carbon dioxide

boiling   woodwind   strings   percussion   conductor

change of state   wealth   cooling   hydrogen

heating   water   ice

guitar   performance   piano   violin

pitch   oxygen

freezing   musician   musical   orchestra   exhibition

opera

discovery   poverty   evaporating   condensing   empire

Look carefully at the words in the Word Bank. Which words could be found in a book about music, which in a book about gases, solids and liquids and which in a book about Victorian Britain? Write the words in the correct places below. Some of the words could appear in more than one book.

Music	Gases, Solids and Liquids	**Victorian Britain**

On a separate piece of paper, write three sentences using some of the vocabulary relating to music, Victorian Britain or gases, solids and liquids.

Teacher's notes

Discuss the words above in relation to the category title cards from page 21. Do the children know what each word means? Can they think of any related words? For example, they could suggest the word 'operatic' in relation to the word 'opera'. Ask the children to sort the words as though they appear in some non-fiction books: Could any of the words appear in more than one of the books? Could any of the words appear in all three books?

Word sorting: music; gases, solids and liquids; Victorian Britain

Word Bank

smog railways canals travel carbon dioxide
rehearse melting notation
boiling woodwind strings percussion conductor
change of state wealth cooling water ice hydrogen
heating
guitar
pitch fluid performance piano orchestra violin
musician opera musical oxygen
freezing evaporating transport exhibition
poverty condensing
discovery industrial empire
tuning invention revolution nitrogen

Look carefully at the words in the Word Bank. Write the words in the correct book below. Some of the words could appear in more than one book.

Music	Gases, Solids and Liquids	**Victorian Britain**

Find some more vocabulary for each book.

Teacher's notes

Discuss the words above in relation to the category title cards from page 21. Do the children know what each word means? To find extra vocabulary for each list, the children could research in the school library or on the internet. They could also consider searching for words related to those on the list: for example, the word 'condensation' is clearly related to the word 'condensing'.

Andrew Brodie: Improving Vocabulary for ages 9-10 © Bloomsbury Publishing Plc 2012

Word sorting: sport, wildlife, travel

Non-fiction

Information

Sport

Wildlife

Travel

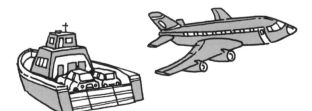

Teacher's notes

Photocopy and cut out the Non-fiction or Information headings and the category title cards to use in conjunction with the activities on the following three sheets. This categorisation activity can be very challenging for some children. It is important that they explain their choices when they are sorting the words - they may make some surprising decisions but ones that are perfectly valid.

Word sorting: sport, wildlife, travel

competitor	spectator	event	Olympic games	tournament
championship	league	pitch	court	stadium
habitat	environment	reproduction	predator	mountain
desert	moorland	prairie	jungle	rain forest
ocean	transatlantic	overnight	time zone	currency
passport	visa	customs	tunnel	tourist

Teacher's notes

Cut out the words and illustrations above and use them in conjunction with the category title cards from page 25. Ask the children to sort the words as though they appear in some school books: which words could be found in a book about sport, which in a book about wildlife and which in a book about travel? Could any of the words appear in more than one of the books? Could any of the words appear in all three books? As an extension activity, ask the children to compose orally two or three sentences that feature some of the words they have discussed. They could write out the best sentences.

Andrew Brodie: Improving Vocabulary for ages 9-10 © Bloomsbury Publishing Plc 2012

Word sorting:
sport, wildlife, travel

Name _____

Date _____

Word Bank

ocean   prairie   overnight   visa   currency

habitat   environment   Olympic games   predator   mountain

competitor   spectator   marathon   species   tournament

exploration   photography   event   commonwealth   relay

runner-up   endangered   voyage

championship   pitch   ornithology   court   stadium

desert   reproduction   transatlantic   jungle   rain forest

passport   league   customs   tunnel   tourist

Look carefully at the words in the Word Bank. Which words could be found in a book about sport, which in a book about wildlife and which could be found in a book about travel? Write the words in the correct places below. Some of the words could appear in more than one book.

Sport	Wildlife	Travel

On a separate piece of paper, write three sentences using some of the vocabulary relating to sport, wildlife or travel.

Teacher's notes

Discuss the words above in relation to the category title cards from page 25. Do the children know what each word means? Can they think of any related words? For example, they could suggest the word 'tourism' in relation to the word 'tourist'. Ask the children to sort the words as though they appear in some non-fiction books: Could any of the words appear in more than one of the books? Could any of the words appear in all three books?

Word sorting:
sport, wildlife, travel

Name _____

Date _____

Word Bank

heptathlon
ocean   prairie   overnight   visa   tunnel   currency
success
habitat   environment   Olympic games   predator   mountain
competitor   spectator   reproduction   species   tournament
exploration   photography   marathon   commonwealth   relay
squad   endangered   event   voyage
runner-up
championship   league   ornithology   finish   stadium
pitch   court
desert   moorland   transatlantic   jungle   rain forest
passport   security   time zone   customs   pentathlon   tourist

Look carefully at the words in the Word Bank. Write the words in the correct book below. Some of the words could appear in more than one book.

Sport	Wildlife	Travel

Find some more vocabulary for each book.

Teacher's notes

Discuss the words above in relation to the category title cards from page 25. Do the children know what each word means? To find extra vocabulary for each list, the children could research in the school library or on the internet. They could also consider searching for words related to those on the list: for example, the word 'ornithologist' is clearly related to the word 'ornithology'.

     Andrew Brodie: Improving Vocabulary for ages 9-10 © Bloomsbury Publishing Plc 2012

Winter

Winter

Nouns

Adjectives

Comparative adjectives

Superlative adjectives

Verbs

Teacher's notes

Photocopy and cut out the Winter heading and the other category title cards to use in conjunction with the activities on the following three sheets. This activity provides lots of opportunities for speaking and listening and introduces important everyday vocabulary. Note that the grammatical terms listed above themselves form useful vocabulary.

Winter

frost	frosty	frostier	frostiest	ice
icy	icier	iciest	bleak	bleaker
bleakest	snow	puddles	slush	skating
darkness	dark	frozen	melting	freezing
misting	wrapping	warming	cooling	blowing
snowing	raining	cold	colder	coldest

Teacher's notes

Cut out the words and illustrations above. Use the cards created from this sheet as prompts for discussion to ensure that this is a speaking and listening activity as well as a reading activity. Encourage the children to talk about what they remember of the winter. Can the children create oral sentences using some of the verbs, nouns and adjectives? Talk about adjectives that make comparisons, giving examples in short sentences: Yesterday was cold. Today is colder. Tomorrow is likely to be the coldest. Explain that the word 'colder' is a comparative adjective and the word 'coldest' is a superlative adjective.

Andrew Brodie: Improving Vocabulary for ages 9-10 © Bloomsbury Publishing Plc 2012

Winter

Name _____

Date _____

Word Bank

frost blizzard frosty bleakest frostier frostiest shorter ice raining

icy snowiest icier snowing iciest bleak bleaker

snowier slush short darker snowfall

shortest wrapping crystals snowy icicles blowing darkest

misting warming snowdrift cooling skating freezing

darkness snow frozen

dark puddles melting

Write the words from the Word Bank in the appropriate places in the table.

Verbs	Nouns	Adjectives

Teacher's notes

Discuss the words in the Word Bank in conjunction with the category title cards from page 29. Ensure that this is firstly a speaking and listening activity although it will provide practice in both reading and writing. Can the children create oral sentences using some of the verbs, nouns and adjectives? Do they know how each of the words could be used in relation to 'winter'? Note that they may use some words as either verbs or adjectives, for example in phrases such as 'the freezing water', the word 'freezing' is clearly an adjective describing the noun 'water' but the same word could potentially be used as a verb, as in 'the water was freezing over'. Encourage the children to put words into phrases or sentences to help them decide what type of words they are. Talk about adjectives that make comparisons, giving examples in short sentences: Yesterday was snowy. Today it is snowier. Tomorrow is likely to have the snowiest weather. Explain that the word 'snowier' is a comparative adjective and the word 'snowiest' is a superlative adjective.

Winter

Name _____

Date _____

Word Bank

blizzard

frost   frosty   bleakest   frostier   frostiest   ice

icy   bleak

snowiest   icier   iciest   bleaker

snowier   snowing   short   snowfall

slush   crystals   darker   holly

snowy   icicles

shortest   warming   blowing   darkest

wrapping   cooling

snowdrift

misting   puddles   skating   freezing

darkness   snow

dark   frozen   melting

evergreen   insulation   snowdrops

shorter   raining

Write the positive, comparative and superlative adjectives from the Word Bank in the appropriate places in the table. One set of adjectives has already been written in the table. Can you think of extra words to write in the table?

Positive adjectives	Comparative adjectives	Superlative adjectives
dark	darker	darkest

Teacher's notes

Discuss the words in the Word Bank in conjunction with the category title cards from page 29. Ensure that this is firstly a speaking and listening activity although it will provide practice in both reading and writing. Can the children create oral sentences using some of the nouns, verbs and adjectives? Do they know how each of the words could be used in relation to 'winter'? Encourage the children to put words into phrases or sentences to help them decide what type of words they are. Talk about adjectives that make comparisons, giving examples in short sentences: Yesterday the weather was frosty. Today it is frostier. Tomorrow is likely to have the frostiest weather. Explain that the word 'frosty' is known as a positive adjective, the word 'frostier' is a comparative adjective and the word 'frostiest' is a superlative adjective.

Andrew Brodie: Improving Vocabulary for ages 9-10 © Bloomsbury Publishing Plc 2012

Spring

Spring

Nouns

Adjectives

Comparative adjectives

Superlative adjectives

Verbs

Teacher's notes

Photocopy and cut out the Spring heading and the other category title cards to use in conjunction with the activities on the following three sheets. This activity provides lots of opportunities for speaking and listening and introduces important everyday vocabulary.

Spring

awakening	migrating	stirring	blossoming	**buds**
flowers	**birds**	warm	warmer	warmest
green	greener	greenest	shoots	**leaves**
bright	brighter	brightest	sunny	sunnier
sunniest	rain	rainy	rainier	rainiest
daffodils	**snowdrops**	**tulips**	blossom	term

Teacher's notes

Cut out the words and illustrations above. Use the cards created from this sheet as prompts for discussion to ensure that this is a speaking and listening activity rather than a reading activity. Encourage the children to talk about what they remember of the spring. Can the children create oral sentences using some of the verbs, nouns and adjectives? Talk about adjectives that make comparisons, giving examples in short sentences: March can have quite warm weather. April is often warmer. May is the warmest month of the spring. Explain that the word 'warmer' is a comparative adjective and the word 'warmest' is a superlative adjective.

   Andrew Brodie: Improving Vocabulary for ages 9-10 © Bloomsbury Publishing Plc 2012

Spring

Name _____

Date _____

Word Bank

rain crocus term blossom brightest

flowers birds warm crocuses warmer warmest

awakening migrating stirring blossoming buds

green daffodils snowdrops tulips shoots renewal leaves

bright sunny fern brighter equinox greenest sunnier

sunniest greener dripping rainy rainier calendar rainiest

Write the words from the Word Bank in the appropriate places in the table.

Verbs	Nouns	Adjectives

Teacher's notes

Discuss the words in the Word Bank in conjunction with the category title cards from page 33. Ensure that this is firstly a speaking and listening activity although it will provide practice in both reading and writing. Can the children create oral sentences using some of the verbs, nouns and adjectives? Do they know how each of the words could be used in relation to 'spring'? Encourage the children to put words into phrases or sentences to help them decide what type of words they are. Talk about adjectives that make comparisons, giving examples in short sentences: Yesterday was rainy. Today it is rainier. Tomorrow is likely to have the rainiest weather. Explain that the word 'rainier' is a comparative adjective and the word 'rainiest' is a superlative adjective.

Andrew Brodie: Improving Vocabulary for ages 9-10 © Bloomsbury Publishing Plc 2012

Spring

Word Bank

rain   term   crocus   birds   warm   crocuses   blossom   brightest
flowers   beautiful   warmer   warmest
awakening   migrating   stirring   blossoming   wonderful   buds
green   daffodils   snowdrops   tulips   shoots   renewal   leaves
fern   bright   sunny   brighter   equinox   greenest   sunnier
sunniest   greener   dripping   rainy   rainier   calendar   rainiest

Write the positive, comparative and superlative adjectives from the Word Bank in the appropriate places in the table. Two sets of adjectives have already been written in the table. Can you think of extra words to write in the table?

Positive adjectives	Comparative adjectives	Superlative adjectives
green	greener	greenest
beautiful	more beautiful	most beautiful

Teacher's notes

Discuss the words in the Word Bank in conjunction with the category title cards from page 33. Ensure that this is firstly a speaking and listening activity although it will provide practice in both reading and writing. Can the children create oral sentences using some of the nouns, verbs and adjectives? Do they know how each of the words could be used in relation to 'spring'? Encourage the children to put words into phrases or sentences to help them decide what type of words they are. Talk about adjectives that make comparisons, giving examples in short sentences: Yesterday the weather was sunny. Today it is sunnier. Tomorrow is likely to have the sunniest weather. Explain that the word 'sunny' is known as a positive adjective, the word 'sunnier' is a comparative adjective and the word 'sunniest' is a superlative adjective. Note that the adjective 'beautiful' cannot be extended to create comparative or superlative adjectives without adding the words 'more' or 'most'.

    Andrew Brodie: Improving Vocabulary for ages 9-10 © Bloomsbury Publishing Plc 2012

Summer

Summer

Nouns

Adjectives

Comparative adjectives

Superlative adjectives

Verbs

Teacher's notes

Photocopy and cut out the summer heading and the other category title cards to use in conjunction with the activities on the following three sheets. This activity provides lots of opportunities for speaking and listening and introduces important everyday vocabulary.

Andrew Brodie: Improving Vocabulary for ages 9-10 © Bloomsbury Publishing Plc 2012

Summer

ripening	blooming	maturing	hot	hotter
hottest	long	longer	longest	heat
length	daylight	evening	dusk	dawn
temperature	midsummer	thunderstorm	lightning	striking
holiday	vacation	cricket	heatwave	relaxation
sunny	sunnier	sunniest	cool	cooler

Teacher's notes

Cut out the words and illustrations above and use them in conjunction with the category title cards from page 37. Use the cards created from this sheet as prompts for discussion to ensure that this is a speaking and listening activity rather than a reading activity. Encourage the children to talk about what they remember of the summer. Can the children create oral sentences using some of the nouns and adjectives? The children should now be familiar with the concept of comparative and superlative adjectives. Can they find the comparatives and superlatives in the set of words? After discussing the comparative adjectives, ask the children to create some more oral sentences using some of these.

Andrew Brodie: Improving Vocabulary for ages 9-10 © Bloomsbury Publishing Plc 2012

Summer

Name _____

Date _____

Word Bank

blue
ripening sunnier maturing bluer shadiest cooler heat
length daylight sunniest evening vacation dusk hotter sunny
hottest blooming longer bluest long dawn
temperature cool hot thunderstorm heatwave shady striking
holiday fun midsummer coolest cricket lightning relaxation
enjoyable shadier sunscreen sunburn burning longest shade

Write the words from the Word Bank in the appropriate places in the table.

Verbs	Nouns	Adjectives

Teacher's notes

Discuss the words in the Word Bank in conjunction with the category title cards from page 37. Ensure that this is firstly a speaking and listening activity although it will provide practice in both reading and writing. Encourage the children to talk about what they remember of the summer. Can they create oral sentences using some of the nouns and adjectives? Can they find the comparative and superlative adjectives? You may wish to take the opportunity to point out how the letter y is replaced by an i when the word sunny is changed to sunnier or sunniest. Discuss the adjective enjoyable: how could this be used in a sentence about summer? How could comparisons be made using this adjective? Hopefully the children will see the need to insert the words 'more' or 'most' to be able to say 'more enjoyable' or 'most enjoyable'.

Name _____

Date _____

Word Bank

blue   sunnier   cooler   heat
ripening   maturing   bluer   shadiest
relaxing   evening   sunny
length   daylight   vacation   hotter
sunniest   shade   longer   dusk
hottest   bluest   long   dawn
temperature   cool   blooming   thunderstorm   heatwave   striking
    shady
hot   holiday   fun   midsummer   coolest   cricket   lightning   relaxation
    sunscreen   longest
enjoyable   shadier   sunburn   burning

Write the positive, comparative and superlative adjectives from the Word Bank in the appropriate places in the table. Two sets of adjectives have already been written in the table. Can you think of extra words to write in the table?

Positive adjectives	Comparative adjectives	Superlative adjectives
shady	shadier	shadiest
relaxing	more relaxing	most relaxing

Teacher's notes

Discuss the words in the Word Bank in conjunction with the category title cards from page 37. Ensure that this is firstly a speaking and listening activity although it will provide practice in both reading and writing. Encourage the children to talk about what they remember of the summer. Can they find the comparative and superlative adjectives in the Word Bank? Discuss the adjective relaxing: how could this be used in a sentence about summer? How could comparisons be made using this adjective? Hopefully the children will see the need to insert the words 'more' or 'most' to be able to say 'more relaxing' or 'most relaxing'. Note that some children may state that relaxing is a verb, which is correct in phrases such as 'I was relaxing on the beach' but here we are using it as an adjective as in 'it was a very relaxing day'.

Andrew Brodie: Improving Vocabulary for ages 9-10 © Bloomsbury Publishing Plc 2012

Autumn

Autumn

Nouns

Adjectives

Comparative adjectives

Superlative adjectives

Verbs

Teacher's notes

Photocopy and cut out the Autumn heading and the other category title cards to use in conjunction with the activities on the following three sheets.

Autumn

decaying	falling	turning	changing	harvest
harvesting	windy	windier	windiest	storm
stormier	stormiest	gale	hurricane	halloween
bonfire	fireworks	damp	damper	dampest
dampness	festival	carnival	seasonal	autumnal

Teacher's notes

Cut out the words and illustrations above and use them in conjunction with the category title cards from page 41. Use the cards created from this sheet as prompts for discussion to ensure that this is a speaking and listening activity rather than a reading activity. Encourage the children to talk about what they remember of the autumn. Can they create oral sentences about the autumn using some of the nouns, verbs and adjectives? Can they find the comparative and superlative adjectives? Do they notice the word ending 'al' in four of the words?

Andrew Brodie: Improving Vocabulary for ages 9-10 © Bloomsbury Publishing Plc 2012

Autumn

Word Bank

arriving   colourful   North   burning

windiest   falling   gathering   turning   stormiest   harvest

harvesting   South   festival   windier   departing   decaying   storm

stormier   returning   changing   gale   hurricane   halloween

bonfire   fireworks   damp   damper   migrating   collecting

dampness   dampest   carnival   colours   windy   seasonal   autumnal

Write the words from the Word Bank in the appropriate places in the table.

Verbs	Nouns	Adjectives

Teacher's notes

Discuss the words in the Word Bank in conjunction with the category title cards from page 41. Ensure that this is firstly a speaking and listening activity although it will provide practice in both reading and writing. Encourage the children to talk about what they remember of the autumn. Can they find the comparative and superlative adjectives?

Autumn

Name _____

Date _____

Word Bank

arriving colourful gathering turning stormiest North burning

windiest foggier falling vicious departing foggy harvest

harvesting South festival windier decaying gale storm

damper penetrating

stormier returning changing surrounding migrating halloween

heavy bonfire fireworks hurricane collecting

biting dampest foggiest sharp autumnal

dampness colours carnival windy seasonal damp thickening

Write the words from the Word Bank in the appropriate places in the table.
Can you think of extra words to write in the table?

Nouns	Verbs	Positive adjectives	Comparative adjectives	Superlative adjectives

Teacher's notes

Discuss the words in the Word Bank in conjunction with the category title cards from page 41. Ensure that this is firstly a speaking and listening activity although it will provide practice in both reading and writing. Encourage the children to talk about what they remember of the autumn. Talk about the individual words in the Word Bank: can the children see how each word can be related to autumn?

Andrew Brodie: Improving Vocabulary for ages 9-10 © Bloomsbury Publishing Plc 2012

Word sorting: mountains, rivers, traffic

Non-fiction

Information

Mountains

Rivers

Traffic

Teacher's notes

Photocopy and cut out the Non-fiction or Information headings and the category title cards to use in conjunction with the activities on the following three sheets. This categorisation activity can be very challenging for some children. They are likely to need some of the specialist vocabulary when working on geography now or in the future.

Word sorting: mountains, rivers, traffic

	summit	route	scale	
peak	ascend			range
chain	oxygen	Everest	Alps	Andes	Rockies
current	fresh	delta	source	mouth	bed
surface	tributary	estuary	channel	meander	pedestrian
congestion	flow	vehicles	junction	intersection	collision
jam	gridlock	motorist	cyclist	direction	highway

Teacher's notes

Cut out the words and illustrations above and use them in conjunction with the category title cards from page 45. Ask the children to sort the words as though they appear in some non-fiction books: which words could be found in a book about mountains, which in a book about rivers and which could be found in a book about road transport? Could any of the words appear in more than one of the books? Could any of the words appear in all three books? Do they understand the use of the word 'scale', meaning 'climb'? As an extension activity, ask the children to compose orally two or three sentences that feature some of the words they have discussed. They could write out the best sentences.

Andrew Brodie: Improving Vocabulary for ages 9-10 © Bloomsbury Publishing Plc 2012

Word sorting:
mountains, rivers, traffic

Name _____

Date _____

Word Bank

highway   range   direction

congestion   oxygen   vehicles   Alps

peak   fresh   ascend   source   scale   Rockies

chain   channel   Andes   bed

current   flow   delta   junction   mouth   pedestrian

Everest   gridlock   estuary   cyclist   meander

jam   summit   tributary   route   collision   surface

carriageway   motorist   intersection   calming

control

Look carefully at the words in the Word Bank. Which words could be found in a book about mountains, which in a book about rivers and which could be found in a book about road traffic? Write the words in the correct places below. Some of the words could appear in more than one book. You may like to add some extra words.

Mountains	Rivers	Traffic

On a separate piece of paper, write three sentences using some of the vocabulary relating to mountains, rivers or traffic.

Teacher's notes

Discuss the words above in relation to the category title cards from page 45. Do the children know what each word means? Can they think of any related words? For example, they could suggest the word 'descend' in relation to the word 'ascend'. Can they think of other words that end with 'ist'? Ask the children to sort the words as though they appear in some non-fiction books: Could any of the words appear in more than one of the books? Could any of the words appear in all three books?

Word sorting:
mountains, rivers, traffic

Name _____

Date _____

Look carefully at the words in the Word Bank. Write the words in the correct book below. Some of the words could appear in more than one book.

Mountains	Rivers	Traffic

Find some more vocabulary for each book.

Teacher's notes

Discuss the words above in relation to the category title cards from page 45. Do the children know what each word means? To find extra vocabulary for each list, the children could research in the school library or on the internet. They could also consider searching for words related to those on the list: for example, the word 'congestion' is clearly related to the word 'congested'.

Andrew Brodie: Improving Vocabulary for ages 9-10 © Bloomsbury Publishing Plc 2012

Word sorting: drama, poetry, art

Non-fiction

Fiction

Information

Entertainment

Drama

Poetry

Art

Word sorting: drama, poetry, art

performance	theatre	audience	actor	director
scenery	stage	script	character	comedy
rhyme	rhythm	verse	writer	poet
sonnet	haiku	limerick	recite	easel
palette	sculpture	painting	print-making	pottery
dance	oil	acrylic	watercolour	clay

Teacher's notes

Cut out the words and illustrations above and use them in conjunction with the category title cards from page 49. Ask the children to sort the words as though they appear in some books: which words could be found in a book about drama, which in a book about poetry and which could be found in a book about art? Could any of the words appear in more than one of the books? Could any of the words appear in all three books? As an extension activity, ask the children to compose orally two or three sentences that feature some of the words they have discussed. They could write out the best sentences.

Andrew Brodie: Improving Vocabulary for ages 9-10 © Bloomsbury Publishing Plc 2012

Word sorting: drama, poetry, art

Name _____

Date _____

Word Bank

performance   prompt   print-making

palette   theatre   painting   rhyme   clay

sculptor   acrylic   actor   character

scenery   rhythm   stage   writer

haiku   audience   script   recite   comedy

sonnet   dance   verse   director   poet

cue   oil   limerick   easel

pottery   talent   watercolour

Look carefully at the words in the Word Bank. Which words could be found in a book about drama, which in a book about poetry and which could be found in a book about art? Write the words in the correct places below. Some of the words could appear in more than one book. You may like to add some extra words.

Drama	**Poetry**	**Art**

On a separate piece of paper, write three sentences using some of the specialist vocabulary related to drama, poetry or art.

Teacher's notes

Discuss the words above in relation to the category title cards from page 49. Do the children know what each word means? Can they think of any related words? For example, they could suggest the word 'performer' in relation to the word 'performance'. Ask the children to sort the words as though they appear in some books: Could any of the words appear in more than one of the books? Could any of the words appear in all three books?

Word sorting: drama, poetry, art

Name _____

Date _____

Word Bank

gallery   prompt   production   exhibition   lighting

palette   performance   theatre   painting   scan   clay

dance   stage   acrylic   actor   character

scenery   rhythm   audience   writer   director

rhyme   haiku   sculptor   script   recite   comedy

sonnet   sculpture   verse   print-making   poet

cue   model   oil   limerick   watercolour   easel

pottery   talent   canvas   metaphor

Look carefully at the words in the Word Bank. Write the words in the correct book below. Some of the words could appear in more than one book.

Drama	**Poetry**	**Art**

Find some more specialist vocabulary for each book.

Teacher's notes

Discuss the words above in relation to the category title cards from page 49. Do the children know what each word means? To find extra vocabulary for each list, the children could research in the school library or on the internet. They could also consider searching for words related to those on the list: for example, the word 'recital' is clearly related to the word 'recite'.

Word sorting: maths, physical education, outdoor adventure

Non-fiction

Information

Mathematics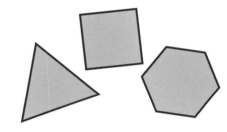

Physical Education

Outdoor Adventure

Teacher's notes

Photocopy and cut out the Non-fiction and Information headings and the title category cards to use in conjunction with the activities on the following three sheets. This categorisation activity can be very challenging for some children. It is important that they explain their choices when they are sorting the words - they may make some surprising decisions but ones that are perfectly valid. You may wish to pay particular attention to the maths vocabulary as the pupils will encounter this in their work.

Andrew Brodie: Improving Vocabulary for ages 9-10 © Bloomsbury Publishing Plc 2012

Word sorting: maths, physical education, outdoor adventure

fraction	decimal	ninth	twelfth	hundredth
percentage	per cent	probable	probability	mathematics
physical	education	competition	health	healthy
healthily	sport	teamwork	cooperation	canoe
kayak	canoeing	kayaking	rock-climbing	archery
surfing	orienteering	windsurfing	perpendicular	parallel

Teacher's notes

Cut out the words and illustrations above and use them in conjunction with the category title cards from page 53. Ask the children to sort the words as though they appear in some non-fiction books: which words could be found in a maths book, which in a physical education book and which could be found in a book about outdoor adventure? Could any of the words appear in more than one of the books? As an extension activity, ask the children to compose orally two or three sentences that feature some of the words they have discussed. They could write out the best sentences.

Andrew Brodie: Improving Vocabulary for ages 9-10 © Bloomsbury Publishing Plc 2012

Word sorting: maths, physical education, outdoor adventure

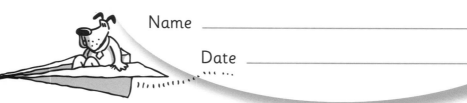

Name _____

Date _____

Word Bank

physical   kayaking   competition   health   per cent

scalene   teamwork   orienteering   windsurfing   rock-climbing

fraction   canoeing   education   hundredth   archery

percentage   compass   healthily   probable

activity

perpendicular   probability   sport   surfing   scaling   surfboard

cooperation

kayak   ninth   twelfth   parallel

healthy   decimal   mathematics   canoe

Look carefully at the words in the Word Bank. Which words could be found in a maths book, which in a book about physical education and which could be found in a book about outdoor adventure? Write the words in the correct places below. Some of the words could appear in more than one book. You may like to add some extra words.

Maths	Physical Education	Outdoor Adventure

On a separate piece of paper, write three sentences using some of the vocabulary from this page.

Teacher's notes

Discuss the words above in relation to the category title cards from page 53. Do the children know what each word means? Can they think of any related words? For example, they could suggest the word 'probably' in relation to the word 'probable'. Which words could be found in a maths book, which in a book about physical education and which could be found in a book about outdoor adventure? Could any of the words appear in more than one of the books?

Word sorting: maths, physical education, outdoor adventure

Name _____

Date _____

Word Bank

kit   currency   numerator

physical   kayaking   competition   health   per cent

scalene   teamwork   orienteering   windsurfing   rock-climbing

fraction   canoeing   education   hundredth   archery

regime   percentage   compass   healthily   probable   fitness

activity

perpendicular   sport   surfing   scaling   surfboard

probability   ninth   cooperation

kayak   decimal   exercise

mathematics   twelfth   parallel

healthy   canoe   muscles

denominator

Look carefully at the words in the Word Bank. Write the words in the correct book below. Some of the words could appear in more than one book.

Maths	Physical Education	Outdoor Adventure
___ ___	___ ___	___ ___
___ ___	___ ___	___ ___
___ ___	___ ___	___ ___
___ ___	___ ___	___ ___
___ ___	___ ___	___ ___
___ ___	___ ___	___ ___
___ ___	___ ___	___ ___

Find some more specialist vocabulary for each book.

Teacher's notes

Discuss the words above in relation to the category title cards from page 53. Do the children know what each word means? Can they think of any related words? For example, they could suggest the word 'competitive' in relation to the word 'competition'. Which words could be found in a maths book, which in a book about physical education and which could be found in a book about outdoor adventure? Could any of the words appear in more than one of the books?

      Andrew Brodie: Improving Vocabulary for ages 9-10 © Bloomsbury Publishing Plc 2012

Outdoor adventure

Outdoor adventure

Verbs

Nouns

Adverbs

Ethan surfs bravely.

Chloe climbs adventurously.

Teacher's notes

Photocopy and cut out the Outdoor adventure heading, the category title cards and the sentence cards to use in conjunction with the activities on the following three sheets. This activity introduces and revises a range of adverbs. Note that grammatical terms such 'adverbs' and 'adjectives' are in themselves useful vocabulary for the pupils.

Outdoor adventure

Fardin	Sam
Nadia	Zak
Isobel	Amy
surfs	climbs
swims	canoes
windsurfs	abseils
cycles	adventurously
bravely	fast
courageously	dangerously
carefully	vigorously
skilfully	carelessly
enthusiastically	skis

Teacher's notes

Cut out the words above and use them in conjunction with the category title cards from page 57. Use the cards created from this sheet as prompts for discussion to ensure that this is a speaking and listening activity rather than a reading activity. Encourage the children to talk about activities that they take part in. If these are not shown on the cards, you may wish to add them. Show the children the two short sentences: 'Ethan surfs bravely' and 'Chloe climbs adventurously'. Ask them to create some similar short sentences using each of the name cards together with a verb and an adverb. They do not have to write the sentences but could do so as an extension activity.

Andrew Brodie: Improving Vocabulary for ages 9-10 © Bloomsbury Publishing Plc 2012

Outdoor adventure

Name _____

Date _____

Word Bank

swimming   surfing   windsurfing

Isobel   Fardin   bravely   Amy   Sam

surfs   Nadia   courageously   carelessly   Zak

swims   carefully   abseiling   canoes   abseils

fast

windsurfs   skilfully   canoeing   dangerously   adventurously

climbs   enthusiastically

cycles   vigorously

takes part in   kayaking   mountain-biking

Write three short sentences using words from the Word Bank.

_____

_____

_____

Write two sentences about an outdoor activity. Remember to use the person's name, a verb, an adverb and any other words you need to complete each sentence.

_____

_____

Teacher's notes

Discuss the words in the Word Bank in conjunction with the category title cards from page 57. Ensure that this is firstly a speaking and listening activity although it will provide practice in both reading and writing. Encourage the children to talk about outdoor activities. If these are not shown on the cards, you may wish to add them. Show the children the two short sentences: 'Ethan surfs bravely' and 'Chloe climbs adventurously'. Discuss the use of the adverb **bravely** to describe **how** Ethan surfs and the adverb **adventurously** to describe **how** Chloe climbs. Explain that the adverb describes the verb but does not necessarily have to be next to the verb in the sentence. Explain that adverbs often end with **ly**. Before the children complete the activities on this sheet, you may like to point out that names of people (countries, towns, etc) are special nouns called proper nouns or proper names and each one always starts with a capital letter. For some sentences they could choose to use the phrase 'takes part in', together with a suitable noun and an adverb.

Outdoor adventure

Word Bank

Isobel	dangerously	bravely	Amy	cycles
enthusiastically	Nadia	courageously	carelessly	abseils
swims	carefully	fast	canoes	adventurously
windsurfs	skilfully	Fardin		surfs
Sam	vigorously	climbs	Zak	

Write the words from the Word Bank in the correct places in the table. Try to think of some extra words to write in each column.

Proper names	Nouns	Verbs	Adverbs

On a separate piece of paper, write three sentences about outdoor activities. Make sure that each sentence includes a proper name, a verb and an adverb. You may need to include other words as well.

Teacher's notes

Discuss the words in the Word Bank in conjunction with the category title cards from page 57. Ensure that this is firstly a speaking and listening activity although it will provide practice in both reading and writing. Encourage the children to talk about outdoor activities. If these are not shown on the cards, you may wish to add them. Show the children the two short sentences: 'Ethan surfs bravely' and 'Chloe climbs adventurously'. Discuss the use of the adverb **bravely** to describe **how** Ethan surfs and the adverb **adventurously** to describe **how** Chloe climbs. Explain that the adverb describes the verb but does not necessarily have to be next to the verb in the sentence. Explain that adverbs often end with **ly**. Before the children complete the activities on this sheet, you may like to point out that names of people (countries, towns, etc) are special nouns called proper nouns or proper names and each one always starts with a capital letter.

Conjunctions

Conjunctions are used to join phrases or sentences together. They make logical links between ideas.

Teacher's notes

Photocopy and cut out or display the title and simple definition. Explain to the pupils that conjunctions are words that have a special job: they join ideas together. There are several different types of conjunction, including coordinating conjunctions (e.g. and), correlative conjunctions (e.g. not only … but also) and subordinating conjunctions (e.g. although). We also make use of adverbs (conjunctive adverbs) such as however, therefore, nevertheless, moreover, meanwhile - these are often used at the start of a sentence, which follows a related sentence.

for	and
nor	but
or	yet
so	both ... and
not only ... but also	either ... or

Teacher's notes

Copy and cut out the words above. Explain to the pupils that conjunctions are words that have a special job: they join ideas together. There are several different types of conjunction, but the activities on this sheet are focused on coordinating conjunctions (e.g. and) and correlative conjunctions (e.g. not only ... but also). However, the emphasis of the work should be on speaking and listening, making use of the conjunctions rather than categorising them into word types. Encourage the pupils to create some oral sentences in which at least one conjunction is used. Note that some words could also be used as prepositions (I had cereal for breakfast) or as adverbs (I haven't finished yet) but the task is to use them as conjunctions (It's a lovely day for the sun is shining; It's a lovely day yet dark clouds are gathering.) Can the pupils think of a sentence for each of the conjunctions on the sheet? You may need to give them some ideas: Not only is your work brilliant but also it was finished on time!

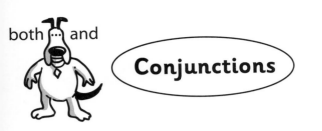

Conjunctions

for	and	nor
but	or	yet
so	both ... and	not only ... but also
either ... or	neither ... nor	although
because	when	until
however	therefore	instead
meanwhile		

Teacher's notes

Copy and cut out the words above. Explain to the pupils that conjunctions are words that have a special job: they join ideas together. There are several different types of conjunction, including coordinating conjunctions (e.g. and), correlative conjunctions (e.g. not only ... but also) and subordinating conjunctions (e.g. although). We also make use of adverbs (conjunctive adverbs) such as however, therefore, nevertheless, moreover, meanwhile - these are often used at the start of a sentence, which follows a related sentence. However, the emphasis of the work should be on speaking and listening, making use of the conjunctions rather than categorising them into word types. Encourage the pupils to create some oral sentences in which at least one conjunction is used. Note that some words could also be used as prepositions (I had cereal for breakfast) or as adverbs (I haven't finished yet) but the task is to use them as conjunctions (It's a lovely day for the sun is shining; It's a lovely day yet dark clouds are gathering.) Encourage the pupils to create some oral sentences in which at least one conjunction is used. Can the pupils think of a sentence for each of the conjunctions on the sheet?

Conjunctions

for	and	nor
but	or	yet
so	both ... and	not only ... but also
either ... or	neither ... nor	although
because	when	until
while	unless	even if
however	therefore	instead
meanwhile	consequently	furthermore
nevertheless	moreover	meanwhile
accordingly		

Teacher's notes

Copy and cut out the words above. Explain to the pupils that conjunctions are words that have a special job: they join ideas together. There are several different types of conjunction, including coordinating conjunctions (e.g. and), correlative conjunctions (e.g. not only ... but also) and subordinating conjunctions (e.g. although). We also make use of adverbs (conjunctive adverbs) such as however, therefore, nevertheless, moreover, meanwhile - these are often used at the start of a sentence, which follows a related sentence. However, the emphasis of the work should be on speaking and listening, making use of the conjunctions rather than categorising them into word types. Encourage the pupils to create some oral sentences in which at least one conjunction is used. Note that some words could also be used as prepositions (I had cereal for breakfast) or as adverbs (I haven't finished yet) but the task is to use them as conjunctions (It's a lovely day for the sun is shining; It's a lovely day yet dark clouds are gathering.) Encourage the pupils to create some oral sentences in which at least one conjunction is used. Can the pupils think of a sentence for each of the conjunctions on the sheet?

Andrew Brodie: Improving Vocabulary for ages 9-10 © Bloomsbury Publishing Plc 2012